T0196891

BABY SIGN LANGUAGE BASICS

songs for little hands
Activity Guide

Monta Z. Briant
and Susan Z

HAY HOUSE, INC.
Carlsbad, California • New York City
London • Sydney • New Delhi

Published in the United States by: Hay House, Inc.: www.hayhouse.com • **Published in Australia by:** Hay House Australia Pty. Ltd.: www.hayhouse.com.au • **Published in the United Kingdom by:** Hay House UK, Ltd.: www.hayhouse.co.uk • **Published in India by:** Hay House Publishers India: www.hayhouse.co.in

All songs written by Susan Zelinsky (Susan Z), except "The Potty Song," "I'd Like a Banana," and "Tea Party," which were written by Susan Z and Monta Z. Briant, and the traditional songs "Old MacDonald," "Itsy Bitsy Spider," and "Three Nice Mice." All songs © 2002, © 2003, © 2004, Mylaboo Music, BMI. For more information: **www.susanz.com**, P.O. Box 151394, San Rafael, CA 94915-1394.

Editorial supervision: Jill Kramer   *Design:* Jenny Richards

Library of Congress Control No. for original edition: 2006937192

ISBN: 978-1-4019-7428-2

1st Edition, June 2008
2nd Edition, January 2023

Printed in the United States of America

This product uses papers sourced from responsibly managed forests. For more information, see www.hayhouse.com.

Also by Monta Z. Briant

Baby Sign Language Basics★

Sign, Sing, and Play!

The Sign, Sing, and Play Kit

★Also available in Spanish

All of the above are available at your local bookstore,
or may be ordered by visiting:

Hay House USA: **www.hayhouse.com**®
Hay House Australia: **www.hayhouse.com.au**
Hay House UK: **www.hayhouse.co.uk**
Hay House India: **www.hayhouse.co.in**

Audio Download Instructions

Thank you for purchasing *Baby Sign Language Basics* by Monta Z. Briant. This product includes a free audio download!

To access this bonus content, please visit www.hayhouse.com/download and enter the Product ID and Download Code as they appear below.

Product ID: 5481

Download Code: VIDEO

For further assistance, please contact Hay House Customer Care by phone: US (800) 654-5126 or INTL CC+(760) 431-7695 or visit www.hayhouse.com/contact.

Thank you again for your Hay House purchase. Enjoy!

Hay House, Inc. • P.O. Box 5100 • Carlsbad, CA 92018 • (800) 654-5126

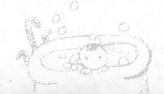

Contents

Introduction

Signing and Singing

Signing along with songs is one of the most effective things you can do to encourage little ones to try new signs themselves. Babies love songs with gestures, because this allows them to participate in them before they can actually sing the words—and that's a lot more fun than just sitting there listening!

When signing with your baby, remember to:

- Get on your baby's level
- Make eye contact
- Sign close to your face
- Say the word as you sign it
- Accompany signs with appropriate facial expressions

Remember that in the beginning, babies will approximate signs to the best of their ability, in much the same way that they approximate their first words. Don't expect perfection—just as most babies will say "wa wa" before they can say "water," you can expect to see your little one doing some "hand babbling" before forming actual recognizable signs.

Most babies will just watch you sign the song at first. Soon, though, they'll begin to realize that there's something *they* can do with their hands, and they may begin to wave them around as you sign the song. Eventually, as their coordination improves and they learn to recognize the lyrics, they'll begin to attempt signing themselves.

How to Use This Book

1. Choose a song to learn. If you're a beginning signer, try one with fewer signs to start.

2. Using the illustrations, practice the signs until you feel comfortable doing them. If you're still

unsure of how a sign is made, you can see a video of it by going to the ASL Browser at **http://www.commtechlab.msu.edu/sites/aslweb/.**

3. Next, try signing while reading the lyrics, signing the words in **BOLD CAPS.**

4. Now you're ready to try it with the music. Turn on the tunes and have fun!

THE SONGS

Bath Time
by Susan Z

Turn on the **HOT!**
Turn on the **COLD!**

WATER in the bathtub! **WATER** in the bathtub!
Turn on the **HOT!**
Turn on the **COLD!**
Make the **WATER** just right!

DIRT on my **FACE!** (Put hands to face or point to face.)
DIRT on my **HANDS!** (Hold up hands to show dirt.)
Let's get a-**WASHING!** Let's get a-**WASHING!**
DIRT on my **FACE!**
DIRT on my **HANDS!**
WASHING the dirt away!

PLAY in the **BATH!**
PLAY in the **BATH!**
Time for my **DUCKY!** Time for my **DUCKY!**
PLAY in the **BATH!**
PLAY in the **BATH!**
BATH time's so much **FUN!**

Signs for "Bath Time"

HOT.
Hand is held like a claw, palm facing the mouth, then drops downward with palm facing down, as if spitting out hot food and throwing it on the floor.

COLD.
The shoulders are hunched, and the clenched hands shake as if shivering with cold.

WATER.
The first 3 fingers form a "W" and tap the chin twice.

DIRTY.

Hold hand under chin and wiggle fingers. (You're in dirt up to your neck!)

WASHING.

The closed fist scrubs the opposite open palm in a circular motion, as if washing something.

PLAY.

Raise the thumbs and pinkies of both hands to form a "Y" hand shape. Shake hands, pivoting at the wrists.

BATH.

The closed fists scrub
up and down the body.

DUCK.

The hand is held near
the mouth, facing out,
while the first two
fingers open and close
on top of the thumb,
like a duck's bill.

Come Down and Play
by Susan Z

BUTTERFLY, BUTTERFLY
Flyin' **UP, UP, UP** to the sky
BUTTERFLY, BUTTERFLY
Come **DOWN** and **PLAY**
BUTTERFLY, BUTTERFLY
Flyin' **UP, UP, UP** to the sky
BUTTERFLY, BUTTERFLY
Come **DOWN** and **PLAY**

LADYBUG, LADYBUG
Flyin' **UP, UP, UP** above
LADYBUG, LADYBUG
Come **DOWN** and **PLAY**
LADYBUG, LADYBUG
Flyin' **UP, UP, UP** above
LADYBUG, LADYBUG
Come **DOWN** and **PLAY**

Come Down and Play, cont'd.

BUMBLEBEE, BUMBLEBEE
Flyin' **UP, UP, UP** in the **TREE**
BUMBLEBEE, BUMBLEBEE
Come **DOWN** and **PLAY**

BUMBLEBEE, BUMBLEBEE
Flyin' **UP, UP, UP** in the **TREE**
BUMBLEBEE, BUMBLEBEE
Come **DOWN** and **PLAY**

Signs for "Come Down and Play"

BUTTERFLY.

The hands fly around
with the thumbs locked
against each other and
the fingers wiggling,
representing a
butterfly flying.

UP.

The index finger
points upward.

DOWN.

The natural gesture—
the index finger
points downward.

PLAY.

Raise the thumbs and
pinkies of both hands to
form a "Y" hand shape.
Shake hands, pivoting
at the wrists.

LADYBUG (BUG).

The thumb rests on the
end of the nose while the
first two fingers wiggle,
like the antennae of an
insect.

BEE.

The "F" hand touches
the corner of the upper
lip, representing a bee
stinging, then turns to
a "B" hand shape and
swats it away.

TREE.

The elbow of the action hand rests on the opposite open palm with fingers splayed open (the "5" hand) to represent the branches of a tree. The hand pivots back and forth at the wrist.

FUN.

Hold the first two fingers of each hand together in the "U" hand shape. Brush action hand's fingers against the tip of the nose, then bring them down onto the fingers of the base hand.

Milk

MILK in the morning
MILK at noon
MILK at night by the light of the **MOON**
MILK is what my **BABY EATS**
MILK is for my **BABY** sweet

(© 2005)

Signs for "Milk"

MILK.

The fist is held sideways and then opened and closed several times, as if milking a cow.

* * * * * *

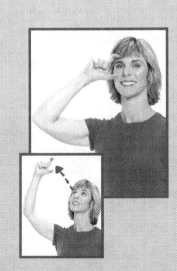

MOON.

A modified "C" hand is made with the thumb and forefinger. It taps the temple, (curving around the eye) then rises up over the head as the signer gazes up at it.

BABY.

One arm cradles
the other and rocks
side to side, as if
rocking a baby.

EAT.

The fingers and thumb,
held together as if
holding a small piece
of food, tap the mouth
several times.

Going to the Zoo
by Susan Z

It's **GRANDMA** and **GRANDPA**'s day to take me **OUT**
We're **GOING** to the zoo where the
MONKEY likes to shout
I hope to **SEE** an **ELEPHANT** raise her trunk up high
I hope to **SEE** a tall **GIRAFFE** as we go strolling by

I used to get **SCARED** whenever I would
hear the **TIGERS** roar
But now I know they were saying **HELLO,** and I'm not
SCARED anymore (shake head **NO**)
NO, I'm not **SCARED** anymore (shake head **NO**)

It's **GRANDMA** and **GRANDPA**'s day to take me **OUT**
We're **GOING** to the zoo where the
MONKEY likes to shout

(© 2004, Mylaboo Music, BMI)

Signs for "Going to the Zoo"

GRANDMA.
The "5" hand is held sideways with the thumb touching the chin. The hand then moves downward and away in two arcs.

* * * * * *

GRANDPA.
The "5" hand is held sideways with the thumb touching the forehead. The hand then moves downward and away in two arcs.

* * * * * *

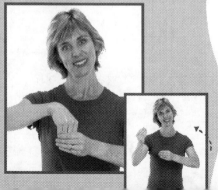

OUT.
One hand moves out of the other.

GO.
Both hands, with index fingers extended, bend at the wrists and point in the direction you're going.

* * * * * *

MONKEY.
The hands scratch up and down on the sides, imitating a monkey.

* * * * * *

ELEPHANT.
Starting at the nose, the "C" hand traces the shape of an elephant's trunk.

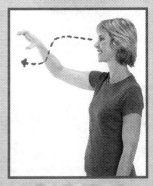

GIRAFFE.

The "C" hand starts at the neck and moves up, tracing the shape of a giraffe's neck.

. . . . . .

SCARED.

The fists face each other, then suddenly move together as the palms open and the fingers shake. A startled expression on the face is important.

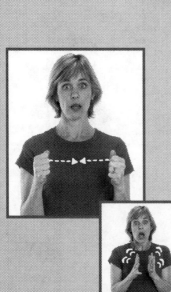

TIGER.

The bent fingers of both hands are pulled across the face, representing a tiger's stripes.

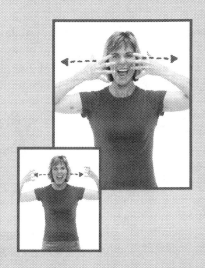

HELLO.

The ASL **HELLO** is like a salute, moving the flat hand out from the side of the forehead. Alternatively, you can just wave.

I'd Like a Banana

by Susan Z and Monta Briant

I'd like a **BANANA, BANANA, BANANA**
I'd like a **BANANA**
MOMMY, may I **PLEASE**

Now I'd like some **MILK,** some **MILK,** some **MILK**
Now I'd like some **MILK**
MOMMY, may I **PLEASE**

I would like a **CRACKER,** a **CRACKER,** a **CRACKER**
I would like a **CRACKER**
MOMMY, may I **PLEASE**

THANK YOU for the **CRACKER** and **MILK** and **BANANA**
Now I think I'm **FINISHED**
THANKS for all of these

(© 2003, Mylaboo Music, BMI)

Signs for "I'd Like a Banana"

BANANA.
Pretend to "peel" your left index finger, as if it were a banana.

MOMMY.
The thumb of sideways "5" hand taps the chin several times.

PLEASE.
The open palm touches the chest and moves in a circular motion.

CRACKER.

The fist of the base hand is held against the opposite shoulder, as the action hand forms a fist and strikes the elbow of the base arm several times.

MILK.

The fist is held sideways, then opened and closed several times, as if milking a cow.

THANK YOU.

The fingertips of the flat hand touch the lips, and then move out and down toward the person being thanked, representing nice words coming from the mouth.

FINISHED (ALL DONE).

Both "5" hands are held with the palms up, then flip over in one swift motion.

In the Morning
by Susan Z

In the **MORNING,** in the **MORNING**

I like to **WAKE UP** early in the **MORNING**

I **JUMP, JUMP, JUMP**

I **JUMP** right out of bed

Oh, my favorite time of day is in the **MORNING**

In the **MORNING,** in the **MORNING**

I like to wake up early in the **MORNING**

EAT, EAT, EAT

It's time for me to **EAT**

Oh, my favorite time of day is in the **MORNING**

In the **MORNING,** in the **MORNING**
I like to **WAKE UP** early in the **MORNING**
SHOES, SHOES, SHOES
I get to wear my **SHOES**
Oh, my favorite time of day is in the **MORNING**

Oh, the **MOON, MOON, MOON** comes out at night
And a shooting **STAR** is a lovely sight,
But I'll be fast **ASLEEP, DREAMIN'** of the time
When I get to see that big **SUNSHINE**

In the **MORNING,** in the **MORNING**
I like to **WAKE UP** early in the **MORNING**
I **JUMP, JUMP, JUMP**
I **JUMP** right out of bed
Oh, my favorite time of day is in the **MORNING**

Signs for "In the Morning"

MORNING.

The base hand rests palm down, just above the elbow of the upturned action forearm, which then rises up to an almost-vertical position. The base arm is the "horizon," and the action arm represents the sun rising.

WAKE UP.

Hold forefingers and thumbs together at the corners of the eyes and then open them up, to indicate eyes opening.

JUMP.

The first two fingers of the action hand form an inverted "V" on the palm of the base hand. The action hand springs up and down, representing legs jumping.

* * * * * *

SHOES.

The thumb sides of the fists tap together, representing someone clicking the heels of their shoes together.

* * * * * *

MOON.

A modified "C" hand is made with the thumb and forefinger. It taps the temple, then rises up over the head as the signer gazes up at it.

STAR.

The two index fingers rub against each other as they point alternately skyward. This represents stars twinkling.

SLEEP.

The palm of the open "5" hand is held in front of the face, then pulls down as the head droops forward (as if falling asleep).

DREAM.

The forefinger touches the forehead, then pulls away as it bends at the knuckle repeatedly.

SUNSHINE.

The "C" hand taps the temple, then rises up over the head as the signer gazes up at it.

Old MacDonald
Traditional

Old MacDonald had a farm
E-I-E-I-O

And on his farm he had a **COW**
E-I-E-I-O
With a **MOO-MOO** here
And a **MOO-MOO** there
Here a **MOO,** there a **MOO**
Everywhere a **MOO-MOO**
Old MacDonald had a farm
E-I-E-I-O

And on his farm he had a **DUCK**
E-I-E-I-O
With a **QUACK-QUACK** here
And a **QUACK-QUACK** there
Here a **QUACK,** there a **QUACK**

Everywhere a **QUACK-QUACK**
Old MacDonald had a farm
E-I-E-I-O

And on his farm he had a **HORSE**
E-I-E-I-O
With a **NEIGH-NEIGH** here
And a **NEIGH-NEIGH** there
Here a **NEIGH,** there a **NEIGH**
Everywhere a **NEIGH-NEIGH**
Old MacDonald had a farm
E-I-E-I-O

And on his farm he had a **PIG**
E-I-E-I-O
With an **OINK-OINK** here
And an **OINK-OINK** there
Here an **OINK,** there an **OINK**
Everywhere an **OINK-OINK**
Old MacDonald had a farm
E-I-E-I-O

Signs for "Old MacDonald"

COW.
The thumb of the "Y" hand rest on the temple, then bends forward at the wrist.

DUCK.
The hand is held near the mouth, facing out, while the first two fingers open and close on top of the thumb, indicating a duck's bill.

HORSE.

The thumb touches the temple, while the extended first two fingers flap up and down together, like a horse's ear. You can use one or both hands.

PIG.

The hand flaps up and down underneath the chin, representing food dripping from the mouth of a pig.

Itsy Bitsy Spider
Traditional, and inspired by Asheba

Oh, the itsy bitsy **SPIDER** went up the water spout
(make **SPIDER** go up)
Down came the **RAIN** and **WASHED** the **SPIDER OUT**
(sign **FINISHED**)
Out came the **SUN** and dried up all the **RAIN**
(sign **RAIN** going up in reverse!)
And the itsy bitsy **SPIDER** went up the spout
(make **SPIDER** go up) **AGAIN**

GO itsy! **GO** itsy! **GO** itsy, **GO**!

Signs for "Itsy Bitsy Spider"

SPIDER.

Pinkie fingers are locked together, and the rest of the fingers wiggle as hands move forward.

RAIN.

The hands, held palms down with fingers spread and slightly bent, make a double downward movement, representing rain falling.

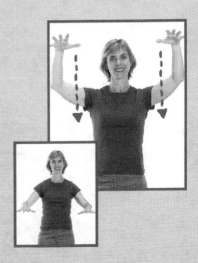

FINISHED.

Both "5" hands are held palms up, then flip over in one swift motion.

SUN.

The "C" hand taps the temple, then rises up over the head.

AGAIN.

The fingertips of the curved action hand come down in an arc to touch the upturned palm of the base hand.

GO.

Both hands, with index fingers extended, bend at the wrists and point in the direction you're going.

I Rest My Head
by Susan Z

When the day is **DONE** (sign **FINISHED**),
it's time for **BED**
I kiss my **BEAR** and **REST MY HEAD** (sign **BED**)

When the **SUN GOES DOWN** in the eve
DADDY reads my **BOOK** to me

When the **MOON** and the **STARS** fill the sky
MOMMY SINGS LULLABIES (sign **MUSIC**)

When the day is **DONE,** it's time for **BED**
I kiss my **BEAR** and **REST MY HEAD, I REST MY HEAD,**
I REST MY HEAD . . . (sign **BED** repeatedly)

Signs for "I Rest My Head"

FINISHED (ALL DONE).

Both "5" hands are held palms up, then flip over in one swift motion.

BED

(Use for **SLEEP/ REST**). Rest your head on your hand as if it's a pillow.

BEAR.

The two "claw hands," crossed over the chest, make scratching motions, like a bear scratching itself.

· · · · · ·

SUN GOES DOWN.

The "C" hand taps the temple, then rises up over the head. Then it sinks slowly down.

· · · · · ·

DADDY.

The thumb of sideways "5" hand taps the middle of the forehead several times. The fingertips may wiggle.

BOOK.

Hold hands flat, with palms together. Open hands like the pages of a book.

* * * * * *

MOON.

A modified "C" hand is made with the thumb and forefinger. It taps the temple, then rises up over the head as the signer gazes up at it.

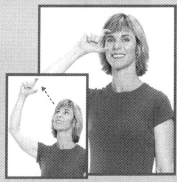

* * * * * *

STARS.

The two index fingers rub against each other as they point alternately skyward. This represents stars twinkling.

MOMMY.
The thumb of sideways "5" hand taps the chin several times.

MUSIC/SING.
The action hand, held on its side, moves rhythmically back and forth over the forearm, which is held in front of the chest.

Tea Party
by Susan Z and Monta Briant

HELLO! HELLO! I'd like to say **HELLO!**
Before we sit and have our **TEA,** I'd like to say **HELLO!**

SIT down. **SIT** down. Would you please **SIT** down?
Before we have our **TEA** party,
we really should **SIT** down.

DRINK tea! **DRINK** tea! It's time to **DRINK** some tea.
Before we take a **COOKIE,** dear,
we should **DRINK** some tea.

MORE tea? **MORE** tea? Would you like **MORE** tea?
There's plenty **MORE** and **COOKIES** too.
Would you like **MORE** tea?

ALL DONE! ALL DONE! The party is **ALL DONE.**
We've had our **TEA** and **COOKIES.**
Now the party is **ALL DONE!**

Signs for "Tea Party"

HELLO.
The ASL sign for **HELLO** looks like a salute. You can also just wave.

TEA.
The "F" hand stirs an imaginary tea bag in a cup that's represented by the opposite "C" hand.

SIT.

The first two fingers of the action hand form a "V" and bend at the knuckles to "sit" on the first two fingers of the base hand.

*   *   *   *   *   *

DRINK.

The signer tips an imaginary glass to the open lips, as if drinking.

*   *   *   *   *   *

COOKIE.

The action hand, held in a "claw" shape, twists around and back again against the opposite flat palm, as if cutting through cookie dough.

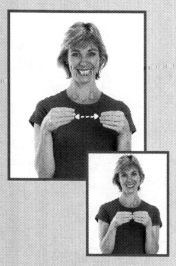

MORE.
The thumbs and fingertips of each hand are held together, and the fingertips of both hands tap together several times. This represents gathering more things together.

FINISHED (ALL DONE).
Both "5" hands are held palms up, then flip over in one swift motion.

Three Nice Mice

Traditional

Three nice **MICE**
Three nice **MICE**
See how they **PLAY**
See how they **PLAY**

They're always polite
When they **NIBBLE (EAT)** their cheese
They always say **"THANK YOU"**
And always say **"PLEASE "**
They cover their noses
Whenever they sneeze
(Cover nose and pretend to sneeze: "Aaah-choo!")

Three nice **MICE**
Three nice **MICE**

Signs for "Three Nice Mice"

MOUSE.
The fist is held in front of the chin as the extended index finger brushes across the nose several times, indicating a mouse's twitching nose.

PLAY.
Raise the thumbs and pinkies of both hands to form a "Y" hand shape. Shake hands, pivoting at the wrists.

EAT.
The fingers and thumb, held together as if holding a small piece of food, tap the mouth several times.

THANK YOU.

The fingertips of the flat hand touch the lips, and then move out and down toward the person being thanked.

PLEASE.

The open palm touches the chest and moves in a circular motion.

The Potty Song
by Monta Briant

Babies need a **DIAPER CHANGE**

Many times each day

But now that I'm a **BIG KID** (sign **CHILD GROWING**)

I know another way

Sometimes when I'm **PLAYING**

I feel the need to **GO**

I run off to the **POTTY**

And there I **SIT** just so

I **SIT** and wait

I take my time

There is no need to **RUSH**

And when I'm **DONE (FINISHED)**

I **WIPE** myself **(WASH)**

And turn around and flush

I don't need a **DIAPER CHANGE**
'Cause I'm a **BIG KID** now (sign **CHILD GROWING**)
I can use the **POTTY**
And **MOM** and **DAD** are **PROUD**

(© 2003)

Signs for "The Potty Song"

CHANGE.
The two fists pivot in opposite directions, changing places.

⋆ ⋆ ⋆ ⋆ ⋆ ⋆

CHILD GROWING.
The flat, downturned palm "pats" an imaginary head down low (**CHILD**), then rises up to show growth.

⋆ ⋆ ⋆ ⋆ ⋆ ⋆

PLAY.
Shake both hands with thumbs and pinkies raised.

GO.

Both hands, with index fingers extended, bend at the wrists and point in the direction you're going.

✦ ✦ ✦ ✦ ✦ ✦

POTTY.

Shake the fist with the thumb tucked between the first two fingers.

✦ ✦ ✦ ✦ ✦ ✦

SIT.

The first two fingers of the action hand form a "V" and "sit" on the first two fingers of the base hand.

RUSH.
The first two fingers of each hand move up and down rapidly.

FINISHED (ALL DONE).
Both "5" hands are held palms up, then flip over in one swift motion.

WASH.
The closed fist scrubs the opposite open palm in a circular motion, as if washing something.

MOMMY.

The thumb of the sideways "5" hand taps the chin several times.

* * * * * *

DADDY.

The thumb of the sideways "5" hand taps the middle of the forehead several times. The fingertips may wiggle.

* * * * * *

PROUD.

The thumb of the "A" hand moves up the chest, indicating the feeling of pride welling up inside.

Where Is My Bear
by Susan Z

WHERE is my **BEAR?**
I thought I put him **ON** the **CHAIR** (sign **SIT**).
WHERE is my **BEAR?**
I thought I put him **ON** the **CHAIR.**
MOMMY, please! **HELP** me!
Oh, **WHERE** is my **BEAR?**

WHERE is my **BALL?**
I thought I **THREW** (sign **THROW**) it down the hall.
WHERE is my **BALL?**
I thought I **THREW** it down the hall.
MOMMY, please! **HELP** me!
Oh, **WHERE** is my **BALL?**

We looked **ON** the chair, **ON** the chair, **ON** the chair,
But still no **BEAR.**
We looked **DOWN** the hall,
DOWN the hall,
DOWN the hall,
But still no **BALL.**

There is my **BEAR.**
It's **HIDING** under the **CHAIR.**
There is my **BEAR.**
It's **HIDING** under the **CHAIR.**
And there's my **BALL.**
It wasn't **DOWN** the hall.
Oh there! I found my **BEAR.**
And my **BALL.**

(© 2003)

Signs for "Where Is My Bear"

WHERE.
Wave index finger side
to side in an arc.

BEAR.
Cross your "claws" over
your chest and scratch.

ON.
One flat hand moves
onto the other.

SIT.
The first two fingers of the action hand form a "V" and "sit" on the first two fingers of the base hand.

••••

MOMMY.
The thumb of the sideways "5" hand taps the chin several times.

••••

ASL HELP.
The flat base hand "helps" the opposite fist go up.

BALL.
The curved, open hands bounce toward each other, as if holding a ball.

THROW.
The hand opens as it moves forward, as if throwing something.

DOWN.

The natural gesture—the
index finger points down.

HIDE.

The "A" fist starts at
the chin, then ducks
under the opposite
palm to "hide."

Baby
by Susan Z

BABY, BABY, BABY
I LOVE YOU so
BABY, BABY, BABY
I LOVE YOU so

I'm gonna **WRAP MY ARMS AROUND YOU (HUG)**
like a **BLANKET**
And keep you **WARM**
I'm gonna **WRAP MY ARMS AROUND YOU (HUG)**
like a **BLANKET**
And **KEEP YOU SAFE (CARE)** from harm
'Cause **I LOVE YOU**

BABY, BABY, BABY
I LOVE YOU so
BABY, BABY, BABY
I LOVE YOU so

Signs for "Baby"

BABY.

One arm cradles the other and rocks from side to side, as if rocking a baby.

I LOVE YOU.

This can be signed as one sign (left) or as three separate signs.

As three signs:

I.	LOVE.	YOU.
Index finger points to self.	The fists cross over the chest at wrists.	Index finger points to other person.

HUG.
The hands hug the opposite shoulders.

* # * * - *

WARM.
The closed fist is held close to the mouth, then opens as it moves away. This represents warm breath coming from the mouth.

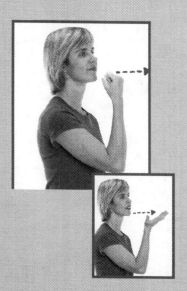

KEEP SAFE (CARE).

Rest one "K" hand on top
of the other at an angle.
(**K** is signed by holding
up the first two fingers,
with the middle finger
slanted in at an angle.)
Then move both hands
in a small circle in
front of you.

65

About Monta Briant

Monta Z. Briant, the author of *Baby Sign Language Basics*, teaches workshops and parent-tot signing classes in San Diego, California, and is available for speaking engagements. She's a member of the Sign2Me™ Presenters' Network and can be reached at **Monta@babysignlanguage.net** For class schedules and other information, please visit: **www.babysignlanguage.net.**

About Susan Z (Monta's sister)

Susan Z (award-winning singer/songwriter/actor) performs live concerts and teaches music classes to babies, toddlers, and parents in the San Francisco Bay Area. She has done numerous national TV/radio ads, independent films, and major motion pictures; has released several CDs; and is a singer on Karaoke Revolution® (Konami®) video games. For info about classes and special bookings visit: **www.susanz.com.**

We hope you enjoyed this Hay House book. If you'd like to receive our online catalog featuring additional information on Hay House books and products, or if you'd like to find out more about the Hay Foundation, please contact:

Hay House, Inc., P.O. Box 5100, Carlsbad, CA 92018-5100
(760) 431-7695 or (800) 654-5126
(760) 431-6948 (fax) or (800) 650-5115 (fax)
www.hayhouse.com® • www.hayfoundation.org

———

Published in Australia by: Hay House Australia Pty. Ltd.,
18/36 Ralph St., Alexandria NSW 2015
Phone: 612-9669-4299 • *Fax:* 612-9669-4144
www.hayhouse.com.au

Published in the United Kingdom by: Hay House UK, Ltd.,
The Sixth Floor, Watson House, 54 Baker Street, London W1U 7BU
Phone: +44 (0)20 3927 7290 • *Fax:* +44 (0)20 3927 7291
www.hayhouse.co.uk

Published in India by: Hay House Publishers India,
Muskaan Complex, Plot No. 3, B-2, Vasant Kunj, New Delhi 110 070
Phone: 91-11-4176-1620 • *Fax:* 91-11-4176-1630
www.hayhouse.co.in

———

Access New Knowledge.
Anytime, Anywhere.

Learn and evolve at your own pace
with the world's leading experts.

www.hayhouseU.com

Printed in the United States
by Baker & Taylor Publisher Services